The New Brown Bag

The Dancing Stones

The Dancing Stones

26 Children's Sermons with Activities

Randy Hammer

THE
PILGRIM
PRESS
Cleveland

The Pilgrim Press, 700 Prospect Avenue East
Cleveland, Ohio 44115-1100
thepilgrimpress.com

Printed in the United States of America on acid-free paper

17 16 15 14 13 5 4 3 2 1

Library of Congress Cataloging-in-Publication Data

Hammer, Randy, 1955-
The dancing stones : 26 children's sermons with activities / Randy Hammer.
pages cm. (The new brown bag)
ISBN 978-0-8298-1955-7 (alk. paper)
1. Children's sermons. 2. Church year sermons. I. Title.
BV4315.H2779 2013
252'.53--dc23

2013028568

Contents

Preface

This book constitutes my fifth published collection of children's sermons, representing ten years of work. It takes its place alongside the last three, *The Talking Stick: 40 Children's Sermons with Activities*, *The Singing Bowl: 26 Children's Sermons with Activities*, and *The Shining Light: 26 Children's Sermons with Activities*, all published by the Pilgrim Press. The stories and lessons in this volume have been created and used at the United Church of Oak Ridge, Tennessee, where the "young members," as we call them, gather in the chancel area every Sunday morning for what I call "some time together." The entries in this work cover such topics as praise and celebration to the Creator, guidance, unity, service to the church and to others, being altruistic, Advent themes, Christmas, Epiphany, happiness, hope, Palm Sunday, Easter, those with disabilities, Pentecost, and Father's (parents') Day.

Generally speaking, my preference in using scripture passages with children is the Good News Translation, designated by GNT, because it is often considered particularly suitable for children. However, occasionally a different translation is preferred, most often the New Revised Standard Version, designated as NRSV. For each scriptural basis of the stories included the suggested translation is noted.

Thank you for your interest in children's religious education and children's sermons in particular. Although some may think that the day for including children's sermons in worship services is past, I strongly disagree. I feel it is important to give children (on their level) in the context of community worship a time for them to come forward and participate and feel a part of the whole. And to that end, I share yet another collection of children's sermons with the church at large.

Introduction

Stones? Why title a book of children's sermons *The Dancing Stones?* Such is a legitimate question. A short answer is that "The Dancing Stones" is the title of the first entry in this collection, since that story has to do with, well, dancing stones. Another part of the answer has to do with the children's sermons series that I have had the privilege of having published these past six years. *The Dancing Stones* as a title just seemed to fit well with my works that have come before: *The Talking Stick, The Singing Bowl,* and *The Shining Light.*

But on a deeper level, stones constitute an important place in our world. Have you ever stopped to think how great a loss it would be if there were no stones in the world for such things as construction of highways, office buildings, places of recreation, even, in some cases, the homes we live in?

But in a real sense stones add so much to the aesthetics of our world. The colors and designs of stones—both outward and inward—add so much beauty and blessing to our lives. Looking at the inside of various kinds of stones that have been cut open can amaze us. Many people wear beautiful, precious stones as articles of jewelry. And have you ever stood amazed when looking at a perfectly formed Japanese garden where every stone is perfectly placed?

Yes, our world would be so much poorer were it not for the many and varied stones that grace our planet.

And so we begin this collection of children's sermons by considering and celebrating stones. Dancing stones.

1
The Dancing Stones
All Creation Gives Praise to the Creator

Scriptures: Psalm 150:6; Luke 19:37–40 GNT

Object for Sharing: A bowl of small, smooth stones, enough to give one to each child

Presentation: This story will work well any time.

Have you ever thought about stones being alive? Or breathing? That seems silly when we first think about it, doesn't it? But some cultures believe that stones in some way are alive too. Certainly at one time in history the materials that some stones are made of were alive. What if we used our imaginations to think about stones and to consider what stones might be thinking or would say if they could speak?

Once upon a time, there were five little stones that lay beside the sidewalk that led into a nursery school for children. Every morning and every afternoon the stones saw and heard all the happy children as they made their way to and from a day of school. The children would laugh and the children would sing. The children would skip and the children would dance. *Oh, if only we could laugh or sing, skip or dance, the way the children do,* the stones thought to themselves. *Then we, too, could give praise to the God who created us. But all we can do is lie around here in the hot sun all day or get smothered by mud puddles when it rains!*

Well, one day the earth started to rumble and shake, rumble and shake. (What do you suppose was happening? That is correct—it was an earthquake.) When the earth started to rumble and quake, the five little stones started to dance up and down. They started to bounce on the ground, jumping first this way, then that. For a full half-minute the little stones danced. And how happy they were that they could dance in glee, giving praise to the Creator who made them, as all creation is made to do.

And that is the story of the day the stones danced.

Follow-up: Using a stone polisher, allow the children to assist in polishing stones. Also, use the opportunity to teach children the natural causes of earthquakes, explaining that they are natural occurrences and should not be looked upon as an "act of God."

2
Something to Show the Way
The Church is Like a Compass

Scripture: Proverbs 3:5–6 GNT

Object for Sharing: A small compass and school backpack

Presentation: This lesson is suggested for the beginning of a new school year.

I bet some of you have seen one of these (show compass). Who might use something like this? (scouts, sailors, hikers, etc.). Good answers! Scouts use them. Sailors use them when they are sailing the seas. Hikers may use them when hiking in the mountains. But what is this used for? To point people in the direction they need to go.

Well, this is called a compass. The special thing about a compass is that the needle always points to the north. So when you look at a compass, you can always know which way is north, but also which way is south, east, and west.

You see, when campers are deep in the woods, if they have a map and a compass, they can always find their way to where they want to go. And when a ship is sailing on the big, wide, open seas, a compass will help the captain stay on course and not just go round and round in circles.

As a matter of fact, a church—this church—is sort of like a compass. Because a church points us in the direction we want to go in life. The church gives us guidance and helps us go the right way when we are faced with decisions about the choices we should make. The church helps us learn how to get along with others. And like the compass that always points to true north, the church always tries to point us to what is true and good.

Since you are starting to school this week, we wanted to give each of you a compass that has a neat clip on it so you can clip it to your backpack. This compass on your backpack can remind you throughout the year of your church, which is always there for you to encourage you and help show you the way in life. So throughout the school year, when you are wondering about the right thing to do or the decision you should make, this compass can remind you of the things you learn here at the church about loving others, doing unto others as you would want them to do to you, and forgiving others, just as you want to be forgiven.

But before we each take a compass, we would like to say a prayer for each of you that you will have a wonderful year of school.

Prayer: We give thanks, Creator God, for each one of these children, and we pray that they might be blessed throughout this new school year. May they learn a lot, may they be kept safe, may they make many new friends, and may this compass always remind them of their church, which cares for them very much. May their school backpacks and everything they will carry in them be blessed throughout this year. And we also say a prayer of thanks and blessing for each of our Sunday school teachers, who will help guide them throughout this year. Amen.

Follow-up: Inexpensive compasses can be ordered online so one may be given to each child to attach to his or her school backpack.

3
A Lock without a Key
We Need Each Other

Scriptures: Ecclesiastes 4:9–10; Matthew 18:20 GNT

Object for Sharing: A (key-opening, not combination) padlock for which there is no key and a few "lost" keys

Presentation: Consider using this lesson on a Sunday when unity is the theme.

The other day I happened to find this beautiful padlock. And I thought to myself, *What a wonderful find!* I was so excited because I have always been fascinated by padlocks, even since I was a child your age. Where might you see a padlock like this one?

Then it occurred to me, what good is this padlock without the key to go with it? Without a key, I can't open it. So as nice as this padlock is, without a key to go with it, it is useless. I might as well throw it away.

But the same thing is true regarding a key. I have a handful of keys here (display an assortment of keys) and I don't have the slightest idea what they go to. Old door locks in houses we lived in years ago, old automobiles that we no longer own, and probably old padlocks that have broken or been lost, like this one.

Well, thinking about a padlock without a key and a lost key without a lock got me to thinking about people. Just as a padlock needs a key, and a key needs a lock to go with it, we need each other. We need each other to help one another. We need each other to make us happy. We need each other because we can do things together that we cannot do on our own.

There is sort of a principle in the universe that it takes at least two to do a lot of things. It takes two people to make a couple. It takes at least two people to make a family. And it takes at least two people to make a church. Jesus said, "Where two or three are gathered in my name, there I am in the midst of them."

So the next time you see a lock without a key or a key without a lock, may it remind you of how they need each other, just like we humans do.

FOLLOW-UP: If you are able, present each child with an inexpensive luggage lock (and key!) that can be purchased at dollar stores.

4

A Basket Case*

Sacrificing for Others Makes Us Feel Good

Scriptures: Exodus 2:1–10; Acts 9:19–25 GNT

Object for Sharing: Some handmade baskets

Presentation: This story will work well on any day when selfless love, service, harmony, etc. is the theme of the day. It could also be used in the context of summer camp or Vacation Church School when basket making is an activity of the week.

One of the oldest forms of arts and crafts in the world is basket making. Can you think of any stories or persons in the Bible involving a basket? (A couple of notable instances include baby Moses being placed in a basket on the Nile River and the Apostle Paul being let down over a city wall in a basket to escape from enemies.)

There is an old story about two basket makers who lived next door to one another. One day the two basket makers were busy making their baskets, trying hard to get them finished before the merchant came to their street to purchase them for his basket shop. One basket maker just about had his baskets finished; he had already put the handles on them. But then he heard his friend next door exclaim, "Oh no! The basket merchant will be here soon to buy my baskets, but I don't have any handles to put on my baskets! What shall I do?"

Well, his friend next door who had already put the handles on his baskets heard what his neighbor had said. So, wanting to help his neighbor in need, the first basket maker removed the handles from the baskets he had finished and took them over to his neighbor and said, "Here, friend, I have these handles left over. Why don't you put them on your baskets?" So the second basket maker gladly took the handles and finished his own baskets, never knowing that his neighbor's baskets were left unfinished.

And even though the first basket maker was unable to sell his baskets that day, he felt good because he had helped his neighbor.

Follow-up: Have basket-weaving materials available so the children can begin making their own small simple basket. For younger children, strips of brown construction paper can be used as well. Discuss some ways that the children might demonstrate acts of selfless love.

* This story is based upon a saying of the Desert Fathers.

5
Whose Job Is It?
Everyone Has a Role to Play

Scripture: Ephesians 4:15–16 GNT

Object for Sharing: A large pitcher or punch bowl filled with water.

Presentation: This story will work well during the season of stewardship.

There once was a little village that learned that their king was coming to pay them a visit. Everyone was so excited! How honored the village officials were that the king was taking time in his busy schedule to see them. So they decided to hold a feast—sort of like a church potluck dinner. It was decided that in order for everyone to offer the king something, every family was to bring a pitcher of the finest wine and pour it into a large container. From this large container the king would be served.

The day for the king's visit finally arrived. The feast began. Then came the moment to draw a glass of wine from the large container. However, when one of the officials turned the spigot, out came—plain water. How embarrassing! The entire village was humiliated. What do you suppose happened? Each villager assumed that all the others would pour in their best wine and that only one pitcher of water would not make any difference. Everyone depended on everyone else to give his or her best, while each one gave the least that he or she could give. And the result was that all of them had dishonored the king.

It is sort of like that in the church. Sometimes we are tempted to assume that everyone else will give her or his best, so we don't have to. But what would happen to the church if all of us expected all the others to give their best and we did nothing? That is correct—nobody would do anything and the church will soon fall apart, wouldn't it?

What are some ways that each of us might give our best? Good answers. When everyone gives his or her best, then everyone can be proud of the church that we build together.

FOLLOW-UP: Draw up a list of the ways that children can help out around the church.

6
Looking Down or Looking Around?
It Is Important that We Focus on the Right Things in Life

Scripture: Matthew 6:25–33 GNT

Object for Sharing: A piece of paper money on the floor

Presentation: This story will work well during the season of stewardship.

Good morning! Have any of you ever found money lying on a sidewalk, street, or parking lot? Most of us have found a few coins in our lives. And when we do so, we consider ourselves lucky, don't we? In fact, we may say to someone who finds money on the street, "Well, this must be your lucky day!" Today I have a story about a child who was about your age who found some money on the street that changed his life forever.

One day Billy was walking home from school. As he looked down at the sidewalk, he spied what looked like a wadded-up piece of money. Billy bent over to pick it up. When he opened it up, he realized that it was a ten-dollar bill. Billy was so excited. He ran home as fast as he could, burst through the front door and exclaimed, "Mom, look what I found! A ten-dollar bill!"

"Wow, Billy, that *is* exciting," his Mom agreed. "What do you think you will do with it?"

"I don't know," Billy replied, "I may just think about it for awhile. You know what? I think I will walk back down the sidewalk and look for more money."

So Billy walked back down the sidewalk, carefully looking all around as he went. Finally he made it to the spot where he had found the money. He didn't find any more. But Billy didn't want to give up. For the next hour or so Billy walked up and down the sidewalks with his eyes focused on the ground in hopes of finding more money.

But the story doesn't end there. Finding that ten-dollar bill changed Billy's attitude forever. From that day on, whenever Billy was out walking, he always looked down at the ground hoping to find more money. Finding more money was all Billy could think about. Every day, everywhere he went, Billy was looking at the ground—the sidewalk, the school playground, the mall parking lot—in search of money.

Now, the sad thing was that by always looking down at the ground Billy was not seeing all the beauty of the world around him. He did not see the beautiful flowers in spring, or the beautiful birds in summer, or the beautiful red and gold leaves in the fall, or the beautiful icicles in winter. He did not see the smiles on the faces of people he passed on the street or in the hall at school. As Billy grew up and went through life, he missed out on so much because he was always looking down at the ground or the floor in hopes of finding more money.

One of the things that Jesus teaches us is that as we grow up we need to be careful of what we are looking for in life. Because the greatest treasures in life cannot be bought. Also, it is important that we look carefully each day to see all the blessings all around us.

Follow-up: Encourage the children to take time to look around the worship or religious education space and make a list of five things they have never before noticed.

7
Preparing the Manger
We Prepare the Way for Jesus' Birth through Acts of Kindness

Scripture: Ephesians 4:32 GNT

Object for Sharing: A small basket and enough small bags of straw so each child can have one

Presentation: This lesson works best on the first Sunday of Advent.

Today is the first Sunday of Advent. Advent is the four-week period before Christmas Day when we prepare our homes and our lives to celebrate the birthday of Jesus. One fun way that we can prepare for the birth of Jesus is to make small, make-believe mangers in our homes.

Here is how we can do it. Each family can take a small basket similar to this one and place it somewhere where everyone in the family can see it, maybe close to other Christmas decorations. Or the basket might be placed on the coffee table or table where you eat your meals.

Now, what might we find in a stable or manger that the animals sleep on? That is correct, hay or straw. Farmers put hay or straw on the barn floor and that is what the sheep and cows sleep on at night. Well, I have a small bag of straw for each of you to take home that you can use to prepare the manger bed for the baby Jesus.

But there is a special way that we will use the straw to prepare the manger bed. Here is how it works: Any time any member of the family sees another member of the family do a kind or helpful deed, then whoever sees it secretly takes one piece of straw from the bag and places it in the manger basket. For instance, Mom might see sister offer to help brother with his homework. That would be a kind deed. So Mom would quietly slip one piece of straw out of the bag and place it in the basket. Or maybe brother would offer to set the table or wash the dishes without being asked to, and Sis sees that. Sis would quietly slip one piece of straw out of the bag and place it in the basket. Or maybe Mom is feeling sad because her best friend moved away and her children give her a big hug and say, "We love you, Mommy." Dad sees this and places a piece of straw in the basket. You get the idea.

The goal is to do enough good deeds to completely fill the basket with straw by Christmas Eve. And if we can do that, then we will have made preparations in our lives to celebrate the birth of Jesus.

Follow-up: Secure beforehand a number of different pictures of the nativity to share with the children. Encourage them to note the differences and similarities in the pictures.

Give a copy of the following instructions to each child, along with a bag of straw.

Instructions for preparing the manger bed for Baby Jesus:

1. Find a small basket and place it somewhere in the home where everyone can see it.
2. Every time someone in the family sees another family member do a kind or helpful act, the person witnessing the kindness secretly takes one piece of straw from the bag and places it in the basket.
3. The idea is for everyone to perform as many kind or helpful acts as possible during the four weeks of Advent so that when Christmas Eve comes the manger basket will be filled with straw.
4. When we have filled the manger basket with straw, then we will have prepared our lives to celebrate the birth of Jesus.

8

The Advent Wreath

The Advent Wreath Invites Us to Celebrate Life

Scripture: Luke 3:1–6 GNT

Object for Sharing: The Advent wreath

Presentation: This story will work best on the first or second Sunday of Advent.

"Hurry up, kids. It's almost time to leave for church. And today is our day to light the Advent candle in the Advent wreath," Mom said, as she held out winter jackets for her two children, Sharon and Jimmy.

"The Ad-WHAT?" Jimmy exclaimed.

"The Advent candle," Mom replied.

"What's *that*?" Sharon asked, with a puzzled look on her face.

"Well," explained Mom, "the Advent wreath is that green circle on the table at the front of the church, near where the minister stands. It has five candles in it—three blue ones, one pink one, and one big white one in the center. The three blue and one pink one stand for the four Sundays of Advent, the four Sundays before Christmas. Each candle stands for a different quality we celebrate during Advent—hope, peace, love, and joy. The pink one stands for love. And the big white candle in the middle of the wreath is called the Christ Candle, and it is lit on Christmas Eve to celebrate Jesus' coming. All the candles remind us that Jesus is the Light of the world. Each Sunday during Advent, a different family lights one of the candles. Today is our turn to light the peace (or whatever Sunday it happens to be) candle."

"But what does the round, green wreath mean?" Jimmy asked.

"Well, for hundreds of years, people have used branches from evergreen trees during the winter time to celebrate life. Have you ever noticed that evergreen trees, such as pine, fir, and spruce, are always green; their leaves don't die like those of other trees? The evergreen wreath reminds us of the promise of everlasting life we have from God."

"But what does Ad . . . Ad . . . , whatever you said, mean?" Sharon quizzed.

"Well, the word Advent means 'coming,' so the season of Advent is the time when we prepare for the coming of Jesus into the world. It's sort of like when we make preparations for a birthday party. It is the time for us to make preparations in our hearts and lives to celebrate the birth of Jesus."

Jimmy and Sharon smiled. And they seemed excited now about putting on their jackets and going to church.

"Okay," Mom said, as they closed the door and walked to their car, "who wants to help read the verse for today, and who wants to help light the candle?"

Follow-up: A fun activity is leading children in making miniature Advent wreaths of green modeling clay or play dough accented by blue or purple birthday or small Hanukah candles.

9

Hand-drawn Gifts

Writing Christmas Cards Is a Way to Bless Others

Scripture: Colossians 4:18 GNT

Object for Sharing: Any number of Christmas cards

Presentation: This story will work best early in December when people are thinking about sending Christmas cards. As the children gather, the presenter can be engrossed in looking at a stack of Christmas cards from a Christmas past.

Oh, good morning! I was just looking through some of the Christmas cards I have received. One of my favorite things on Christmas Eve or Christmas Day is looking at the picture on the front and reading the verse on the inside of each one of the cards we receive.

Did you know that the custom of sending Christmas cards began about 170 years ago? It is thought that the first Christmas cards were hand-drawn by an English artist named John Horsley in 1843. The picture he drew on his cards was a smiling family sitting around a dinner table. Then on each side of the card were scenes depicting acts of kindness.

Today, there are hundreds of different kinds of Christmas cards from which we can choose, from ones that don't cost very much at all to very expensive ones. I like cards that show beautiful churches in snow scenes and ones that have birds sitting on snow-covered trees (or whatever the presenter's favorite card scene might be).

Sending Christmas cards is one of the simple ways that we can bless the lives of others. There is nothing quite like getting a handwritten Christmas card from someone far away. And a handwritten card that we might send could really brighten someone else's day, especially someone who is sad, ill, or alone.

So maybe you could talk with your parents and together you could think of someone who might really be made happy by a Christmas card you could send. You might want to send a card purchased at a store, like one of these. Or even better, like John Horsley, you could draw your own Christmas card and write your own verse inside.

Follow-up: Provide the children with a variety of ready-made Christmas cards from which they might pick one to send, but also provide some folded cardstock or construction paper and colored markers so they can design their own cards if they prefer. Also provide appropriately sized envelopes and maybe even a postage stamp for mailing each card.

10

Away in a Manger

"Away in a Manger" Is a Favorite Christmas Hymn

Scripture: Luke 2:1–7 GNT

Object for Sharing: A manger bed and "Baby Jesus" (doll)

Presentation: This will work any time before or just after Christmas Day. A nice alternative is for the presenter or someone else to play the song on the guitar.

What is your favorite Christmas carol? (Give opportunity for answers.) Well, a favorite Christmas carol for many children, and for some adults, is "Away in a Manger."

For a long time people thought that "Away in a Manger" was written by a great church leader named Martin Luther who lived 500 years ago. But today many people think the carol was written *to honor* Martin Luther when the church celebrated the 400th anniversary of his birth in 1883. When the hymn was first published in a hymnal, it only had the first two verses. Someone added the third verse a few years later.

Do you know what a "manger" is? Sometimes when people speak of a manger they mean the place where the animals slept. But many people believe "manger" means the feed trough, a box made out of wood, where the cattle were fed. That is where baby Jesus was laid after he was born.

What kind of animals do you think might have been there with Jesus in the place where he was born? Those are all good answers. Of course, the Bible doesn't really say which animals were there, but the Christmas carol "Away in a Manger" mentions cows, and there probably were cows there, and maybe some sheep, and maybe a donkey or two.

How about we sing the first two verses of the carol together? Would you like that?

Follow-up: Invite children to create a picture with crayons or paints of their idea of the manger bed and place where Jesus was born.

11

Stocking Surprise

Christmas Stockings Originated Long Ago with Nicolas

Scripture: Proverbs 14:31 GNT

Object for Sharing: A woman's sock or stocking

Presentation: This story is intended for the Sunday just before or the Sunday just after Christmas Day, or it could be used on Christmas Eve.

Has anyone hung up a stocking for Christmas? What does your stocking look like? (Give time for answers.) I have brought a stocking with me this morning. Does your stocking look anything like this?

Well, you know that long ago, when the custom of hanging up stockings on Christmas Eve began, the first stockings didn't look anything like Christmas stockings we see today. The first stockings were real stockings or socks. One story goes like this.

A long time ago, there was a preacher and leader in the church whose name was Nicolas. Now Nicholas was a very kind and generous man who went about helping out those who were poor. One story goes that there were three sisters who wanted very much to get married. But back in those days when girls got married, their fathers had to give money, called a dowry, to the man they were to marry. But the father of these three daughters was very poor, so they didn't have a dowry.

Well, one night the three daughters washed their stockings (they probably only had one pair) and hung them up by the fireplace to dry. Later that night, when the daughters were fast asleep, Nicholas came along and threw gold coins through the window, and the coins landed in the stockings hanging by the fireplace. So when the girls got up the next morning, they found gold coins in their stockings. Now they had the money to get married.

From that night when Nicholas threw the gold coins in the sisters' stockings grew the custom of hanging up stockings on Christmas Eve in hopes that St. Nicholas will fill them with Christmas treats and toys.

FOLLOW-UP: Have gold chocolate coins in your stocking to share with the children as they go.

12

January: Looking Back, Looking Forward

In January We Learn from Our Mistakes and Resolve to Do Better in the Future

SCRIPTURE: Philippians 3:12–13 GNT

OBJECT FOR SHARING: Picture of Janus

PRESENTATION: This story will work best the first Sunday of the New Year.

Who knows what month it is? Correct, it is January. Does anyone know where the name January comes from? It comes from a figure in ancient Roman mythology or literature whose name was Janus. Now, there was something unique about Janus. Janus was always depicted as having two heads that faced in opposite directions. One head looked back at the old year, and the other looked forward to the new year. According to a legend, Janus received the gift to see both the past and future because of the hospitality he had shown.

In Roman literature, Janus was the keeper of gates, doors, time, endings, and new beginnings. So it seemed appropriate to those who devised our calendar that this month be named January after Janus.

There are some things we can learn from Janus. As the old year ends, we tend to look back and think about all we did—both the good and the not so good. If we allow ourselves, we can learn from the past and the mistakes we made and determine that we will try to do better. Then, as we begin a new year, like we are doing this week, we can determine to be the best persons we were created to be. Like

Janus, we look back and learn, and we look forward and set goals.

An early Christian leader named Paul wrote something like this. Paul said that he tried to forget about what was behind him and all the mistakes he made. It is not good to sit around and worry all the time about our mistakes. But then Paul said, "I do my best to reach what is ahead."

So, as we begin this month of January, we take a little time to look back and learn from the past. But then we turn and look ahead to the new year and all the possibilities that lie before us.

Follow-up: Invite the children to share some mistake they might have made during the past year that they can learn from so as to do better in the coming year.

13

Turn on Your Light

Having Light Is Not Enough

Scripture: Luke 2:28–32

Object for Sharing: A windup flashlight

Presentation: This lesson is intended for the season of Epiphany.

I want to share something with you that I received for Christmas. Have you seen one of these? It is a special kind of flashlight. I had not seen one until someone surprised me with this one. What makes this flashlight unique is you never have to put batteries in it. Instead, you just wind it up, like this. Isn't that great? It is filled with light potential. Isn't this a neat flashlight? (Don't turn on the flashlight yet.) And look at the light it throws off! Wow!

What's wrong? It's not on? Does that really matter? Isn't the fact that it is a neat flashlight enough? Isn't the fact that it has all kinds of light potential enough? You mean I have to actually turn it on? Like this (turn on flashlight and show its light on some prominent object)? I am being silly and teasing you. Of course I have to turn on the flashlight if it is going to be of any use to me.

But you know, there may be a great spiritual truth in all of this. Each of us is walking around every day with light potential within us. But just because we have it doesn't mean that we are showing it or making good use of it. Just as I have to make a point to turn the flashlight on and let it shine, we have to make a point to turn our

Christ lights on and let them shine. And the light of Christ is the love of God that we let shine through us.

Do you remember the song, "This little light of mine, I'm gonna let it shine"? We let our light shine when we are intentional about being loving, forgiving, compassionate, and kind to everyone we meet.

So, let's not just carry around the light unused. Let's determine to put our Christ light out there (turn on the flashlight) and let it shine!

Follow-up: Explore with the children practical ways that they may "let their light shine" by being loving, compassionate, and kind.

14

Be Careful What You Say

Sometimes Our Words Come Back to Haunt Us

Scriptures: Ecclesiastes 10:20; Luke 12:3 GNT

Object for Sharing: A plastic or fake parrot in a cage, or a real one in a cage (for the brave of heart)

Presentation: This story will work well anytime.

Can anyone tell us what a parrot is? That is correct—a parrot is a bird that can be trained to talk. Well, about fifty years ago, there lived a great man who dedicated his life to helping others as a medical doctor in a small hospital he built in Africa. His name was Albert Schweitzer. Dr. Schweitzer told a story about a family he knew that owned a parrot. The family tried for months to teach their parrot to say, "Good day." But the parrot would not say it. After awhile, the family got so angry with the parrot that they told him how stupid he was. "What an idiot you are!" they screamed at the parrot. But the parrot just remained silent.

Then one day a very important church leader came to the family's house for dinner. When the important church leader saw the parrot, he went over to its cage, stroked its neck, and then said, "What a beautiful bird you are." The parrot looked at the great church leader, and then it said, "What an idiot you are!"

A message we see in the Bible in a number of places is that we should always be careful what we say. One wise man wrote, "Don't criticize the king, even silently, and don't criticize the rich, even in the privacy of your bedroom. A bird might carry the message and tell them what you said" (Ecclesiastes 10:20).

You see, as the Bible verse and story shows, it always pays to think before we speak, because someday our words might come back to embarrass us, or even get us into trouble.

Follow-up: If possible, show a short, funny (and appropriate) clip from the Jim Carrey movie *Liar, Liar*.

15
Making Things Right
When We Make a Mistake, It Is Important That We Make Things Right

SCRIPTURE: 1 Peter 3:16–17 GNT

OBJECT FOR SHARING: An old, worn, weathered book, if one is available

PRESENTATION: This lesson will work well the second Sunday of February.

Once upon a time, there was a boy who loved books and loved to read. Is there anyone here who loves books and loves to read? Yeah, me too. Well, this young man borrowed from a neighbor a book about the life of George Washington. The boy took the book home and read into the night, and then when he got tired he laid the book upon the shelf. Well, that night a rainstorm came through, and it rained into the house and onto the book. The book was ruined. The cover and the pages were all soggy and stained.

The boy who had borrowed the book felt terrible about it. So the next day he went to see the book's owner and he explained what had happened. The boy said, "I've damaged your book a good deal without intending to, and now I want to make it right with you. What shall I do to make it good? But I have got no money to pay for it."

"Well," the owner of the book said, "come and work for me for three days, and the book is yours."

"Work three days!" the boy said, "And the book will be mine?" The boy was as joyous as could be. He would gladly work three full days so he could own the book that told about the life of his greatest hero, President George Washington.

You know, there is a lot that we can learn from this story about Abraham Lincoln. First, he was a hard worker. Second, he loved to read and learn. And third, and this is really what I think is important, Abe Lincoln always tried to do the right thing. And he showed that he did the right thing in working off the book that was damaged while in his care.

Follow-up: Brainstorm stories of other famous persons who followed their consciences to do the right thing.

16

In Search of Happiness

Happiness Is as Close as Those around Us

Scripture: Philippians 2:1–4 GNT

Object for Sharing: A backpack containing food items and a water bottle

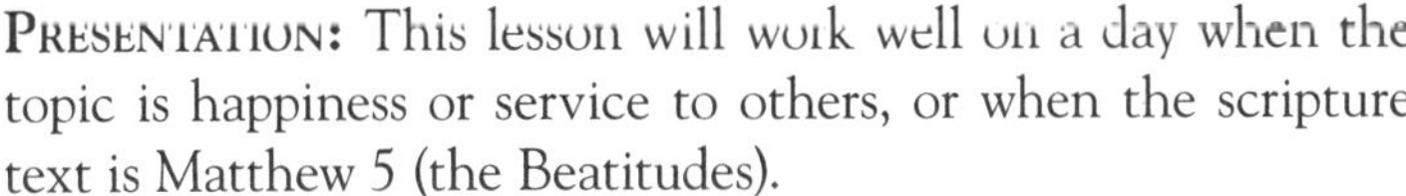

Presentation: This lesson will work well on a day when the topic is happiness or service to others, or when the scripture text is Matthew 5 (the Beatitudes).

Once upon a time, a young man named Johnny woke up one morning and decided that he was not happy. Even though Johnny lived in a nice house, had plenty of food to eat, nice clothes to wear, and plenty of toys to play with, he was not happy. And so Johnny decided that he was going to leave home in search of happiness. So he filled his backpack with food to eat and water to drink, and he set off down the road.

Johnny had not traveled far down the road when he came upon a little girl who was sitting beside the road crying because her bicycle had broken. Johnny was pretty good with bicycles, so he stopped to help. The chain had come off. In no time at all, Johnny had the chain back on, and the little girl hopped on her bike and peddled off down the road smiling. Seeing her smile made Johnny smile too.

A little farther down the road, Johnny came upon a beggar who was holding a cardboard sign that read "Out of work—in need of food." Johnny felt sorry for the beggar, so he reached in his backpack and pulled out a peanut butter sandwich and an apple and gave them to the man. Tears formed in the beggar's eyes, and then he smiled, and Johnny smiled back.

A mile or so farther down the road, Johnny came upon a woman who was struggling to rake the leaves off her small, front lawn. Johnny removed his backpack and offered to help. "I would be happy to rake your leaves for you if you like," Johnny said to the woman, who sort of reminded him of his grandmother, who had just celebrated her eightieth birthday. "Oh, what a fine young man," the woman said. "That would be nice." So in no time at all Johnny had the leaves raked and bagged. When he finished, the woman invited him to sit on her front porch to have some cookies and a glass of milk. While he ate the cookies and drank the milk, the two talked about all kinds of things—books both of them had read, favorite subjects in school, baseball, their favorite holiday of the year, and more. As they talked, both Johnny and the woman smiled a lot. And all of sudden, Johnny realized that he was happy. In fact, it occurred to him that he had been happy all day, ever since he had helped the little girl repair her bike.

Soon it would be getting dark, so Johnny decided he had better start back home. He had gone in search of happiness, and he had found it. Happiness, he had learned, is in helping other people who need help, sharing with those who are in need, and talking and smiling and connecting with others. As long as he could be with and reach out to other people, Johnny decided, he need not look anywhere else for happiness.

Follow-up: Encourage the children to share times when they were really happy (perhaps at holiday gatherings such as Thanksgiving or Christmas, or a birthday party). Try to determine what it was about that occasion that actually contributed to a sense of happiness.

17
The Great Knitter
God Works to Make Our Lives Beautiful

Scripture: Psalm 139:13–14 NRSV

Object for Sharing: A knitted or crocheted article of clothing, such as a prayer shawl

Presentation: This story will work well during the season of Lent or on a day when service to others is being emphasized.

You see that we have brought today a handmade shawl. It takes a lot of skill and a lot of hours to make something like this beautiful article of clothing.

But there aren't very many of us who are perfect when it comes to knitting or crocheting something as beautiful as these pieces. Sometimes a mistake can be made. Maybe the wrong color of yarn is used when another color should be used. Or maybe the wrong kind of stitch is put in. But the person who is skilled in knitting or crocheting often can work the mistake into the pattern of the piece so that it is never noticed. In fact, sometimes mistakes can be turned into something that is even more beautiful than the object would have been originally.

There are a couple of places in the Bible where God is likened to a Great Knitter or Great Weaver who works to knit or weave our lives into something beautiful. One verse in the Bible says, "you knit me together."

But we all know that none of us is perfect. Sometimes we make mistakes, don't we? Sometimes we do things that are not very beautiful. But if we let God help us, even those mistakes that we make or those unbeautiful things that we sometimes do can be turned into something good. We can learn from and grow stronger from our mistakes. And with the help of God, the Great Knitter, we can make our lives even more beautiful.

Follow-up: Share with the children the growing practice of prayer shawl ministry, which can easily be accessed on the Internet.

18
Climbing Out of a Hole

Friends and Determination Can Help Us Overcome Problems

Scripture: Jeremiah 38:1–13 GNT

Object for Sharing: Picture of a donkey

Presentation: This lesson will work well during Lent.

There is an African story about a donkey that fell into a deep well. The villagers had no way of lifting the donkey up out of the well, so they decided the best thing to do was just to fill in the well and bury the donkey by covering him with dirt and sand. There was only one problem—the donkey was still alive.

Well, the villagers began to shovel dirt and sand down into the well. Every time the dirt and sand fell on the donkey's back, he just shook it off, and the dirt and sand fell under his feet. Every time they threw dirt in, the donkey shook it off. And every time the donkey shook the dirt and sand off, the hole filled up under his feet a little more. Eventually the villagers threw in enough dirt and sand that the donkey was raised up through the well and was able to walk out freely onto level ground.

There is another story in the Hebrew book of Jeremiah of how Jeremiah's enemies once threw him down into a muddy well. But Jeremiah also had friends who begged the king to let them get Jeremiah back out of the well. The king agreed, so they tied together a bunch of old rags and made a rope and pulled Jeremiah back up to safety.

None of us probably will ever fall or be put into a well in the ground. But sometimes things happen to us in life that can sort of make us feel like we have fallen into a deep, dark hole. And sometimes we may feel that we are all alone in our problem. But if we look around, it is likely that there are others around us, friends and family members God has given us, who can help us with our problem, just like Jeremiah's friends helped him and the villagers helped the donkey get back up out of the well.

Likewise, we will often have the opportunity to help others who have problems, just as the villagers helped the donkey and Jeremiah's friends helped him.

Follow-up: Consider sharing the story of Joseph (Genesis 37:12ff; Genesis 45) and how his jealous brothers threw him into a pit and then sold him into Egyptian slavery. Be sure to include the part where Joseph says God turned what had happened to him into something good, and share how "bad things" that sometimes happen to us can often become great learning experiences and can often have good outcomes.

19
Unexpected Beauty from Ugly Surroundings
The Lotus Blossom Is a Symbol of Life

SCRIPTURE: Luke 12:27 NRSV

OBJECT FOR SHARING: A photograph or painting of a lotus blossom

PRESENTATION: This story will work well on a day when consideration is given to how we respond to tragic events and trouble.

One of the most beautiful—and fascinating—symbols of life is the lotus blossom, or more commonly known to us, perhaps, the water lily. Can anyone tell us about the lotus blossom? Correct. The lotus blossom or water lily is a beautiful white flower that rests on top of a dark, muddy body of water. The dark, muddy, murky body of water itself reminds us of life and all its darkness and uncertainty. Life is not always beautiful and happy, you know. Sometimes life can be unhappy. Someone might be healthy and happy today only to be facing some great trouble or sadness tomorrow.

When you stand on the bank of a muddy farm pond and try to look through the dark waters to the bottom below, you never know what is down there in the murky mire, do you? We look into the muddy waters with a certain amount of fear and uncertainty. So it also sometimes as we look at life.

But then, there is the beautiful lotus blossom or water lily that rests above the dark, muddy, murky waters, a lovely white flower that remains beautiful and unstained, despite the source from which it springs.

The roots of the lotus blossom descend through the dark, murky waters to the floor of the pond, where they feed on the mold and decay of leaves and other earthy matter. Indeed, the beauty of the water lily would not be possible were it not for the death and decay at the bottom of the pond that give it life.

The lotus blossom or water lily becomes, then, a fitting symbol of the human soul or spirit that rises above the muddy waters of life, above sickness and suffering, human weakness and uncertainty, trouble and death.

But as with the water lily, many people are able to rise above their difficulties and troubles to make something beautiful of their lives. What is it, do you suppose, that enables them to do that? (Some answers might include courage, determination, faith, etc.).

So whenever life seems dark, or troublesome, or discouraging, let us try to remember the lesson of the lotus blossom and how it grows out of dark, frightening surroundings to produce something beautiful for the world.

Follow-up: Explore with the children how the lotus blossom serves as a religious symbol for other faiths, especially Buddhism.

20
Wave Those Pom-Poms
Why We Have Palm Branches on Palm Sunday

Scripture: John 12:12–13 GNT

Object for Sharing: High school or college pom-poms

Presentation: This lesson is intended for Palm Sunday.

"Yeah! Go! Whew-hoo!" (Wave pom-poms all the while.) Have you ever done something like that before? Where would you do something like that? That's right, at a high school or college football game. Or maybe while watching a parade.

On a Sunday long ago, there was a parade into the city of Jerusalem. The parade master was none other than Jesus himself, who led the procession while riding on a donkey. Some of Jesus' disciples followed behind him, while others lined up alongside the road and waved pom-poms. Well, they didn't really wave pom-poms, did they? What did they wave? Palm branches, from palm trees. It sounds almost the same but is spelled differently. They cut palm branches from the trees, and some of them laid them on the road in front of Jesus and others waved them in the air while they shouted, "Hosanna! Praise God! Way to go, Jesus!"

You see, people who really got to know Jesus realized that there was something different about him. And so, when he rode into Jerusalem that day, they gathered to celebrate him and the message that he taught.

To remember that day, we wave palm branches every year on the Sunday just before Easter. Today is a day of celebration. So let's celebrate!

Follow-up: Lead the children in waving their "palm palms" as they leave the worship space.

21
Surprising Flowers
From Bleak Circumstances Beautiful Things Can Grow

Scripture: Isaiah 35:1–2 GNT

Object for Sharing: Photograph of a desert wildflower

Presentation: This lesson is intended for early spring.

Do you like wildflowers? I love wildflowers. Wildflowers are one of the most beautiful things in all creation.

While searching the Internet for wildflowers this past week, I ran across this beautiful flower (display wildflower photograph so that all can see it). Isn't it beautiful? Would anyone like to guess where this wildflower might be found? Those are all good guesses. Actually, this particular wildflower grows in the desert. It is called the Desert Globemallow (or the name of whatever desert flower you have chosen). It grows in the hot, dry, sandy, rocky desert. That's sort of amazing, isn't it? Because usually when we think of deserts we don't think about anything growing there, do we? But a fact that I found very surprising is that there are dozens and dozens of different kinds of beautiful wildflowers that grow in the desert. They have been able to adapt even though it's very hot and there is little rain. Even the desert can be a beautiful place—if we know how to spot the beauty.

A lesson that I learn from desert wildflowers is that beauty and goodness can grow up just about anywhere. God's vast creation is full of different kinds of beauty that help bless our lives.

If such beauty can grow in an environment as difficult as the hot, dry, sandy, rocky desert, just think of the magnificent beauty that can grow forth from you and me.

Follow-up: Assist the children in researching more desert flowers in wildflower books or on the Internet. Invite the children to select a flower that they like best and share the reasons why.

22

Pay It Forward

Doing Something Nice Can Set Off a Chain Reaction

Scripture: Galatians 6:10 GNT

Object for Sharing: A large water toy

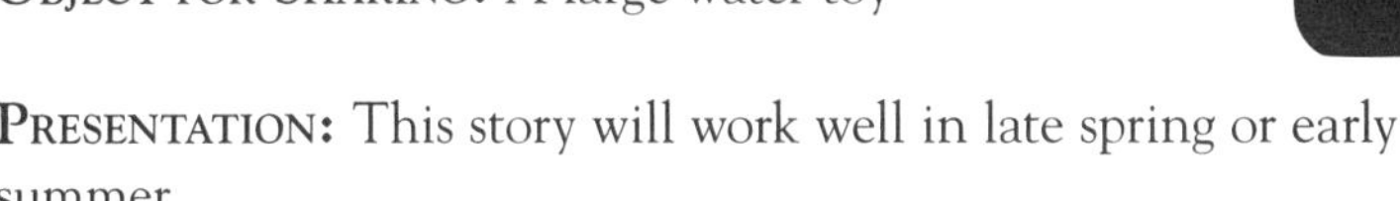

Presentation: This story will work well in late spring or early summer.

Brandon walked into the local pharmacy and went straight to the toy isle. He knew just what he wanted—a giant water toy. It was getting hot outside, and he was ready to play in the water. When he found the one he wanted, he hurried to the check-out line to pay for it. The owner, Mr. Clark, knew his name. Brandon's family had been coming to Clark's Pharmacy for years.

"What you got there, Brandon?" Mr. Clark asked, as he ran the toy across the scanner.

"A squirt gun!" Brandon exclaimed excitedly.

"Oh, somebody is going to get wet," Mr. Clark smiled. "That will be $6.59." Brandon dug in his pocket and put all the money he had on the counter. One, two, three, four, five dollars, and two quarters. Five dollars and fifty cents was all he had. A worried look covered Brandon's face.

Seeing the disappointment in Brandon's eyes, Mr. Clark reached in his own pocket and took out a dollar bill and nine pennies and added them to the rest of the money on the counter. "There we go," Mr. Clark said. "Now we're covered."

Brandon didn't know what to say. "Uh, uh, thanks, Mr. Clark," he finally was able to get out. "I'll pay you back the rest, I promise."

"I tell you what, Brandon," Mr. Clark said. "Pay it forward."

"Pay it what?" Brandon said. He didn't understand.

"Pay it forward. That means since I did something nice for you, now you go and find an opportunity to do something nice for someone else, and then ask them to do the same. Together we will set off a chain reaction of nice deeds. Get the picture?" Brandon did get the picture. He picked up his toy and happily skipped down the street wondering what kind of a nice deed he might do for someone else.

It didn't take long. Just a couple of blocks down the street, Brandon came upon another boy about his age who was struggling with his bicycle and a bag of groceries. His bike had broken down, and he was struggling to push the bike and hold onto the bag of groceries. Here was an opportunity for Brandon to pay it forward. "Hey, how about I help you?" Brandon said. "My name is Brandon; what is yours?"

"Paul," the boy said reluctantly. He wasn't sure whether to trust Brandon or not.

"I need to pay it forward," Brandon assured him.

"Say what?" Paul replied, puzzled.

"Pay it forward. Someone did something nice for me, so now I want to do something nice for you. I want to help you with your bike and groceries. Then you can pay it forward to someone else.'

"Well, okay. I guess," Paul agreed. So Brandon helped Paul home with his bike and groceries, and then Brandon went on his way home.

A little later that day, Paul happened to be looking out his kitchen window when he saw his neighbor, an elderly woman, trying to start her lawnmower to cut the grass. She was having trouble pulling the starter rope. He remembered what Brandon had said about paying it forward. Paul ran out the kitchen door and into the lawn next door.

"Here, Mrs. Walker, let me do that for you," Paul said.

"Why, what a nice boy," Mrs. Walker smiled. "I will see that you are well paid."

"Oh, that won't be necessary," Paul said. "Just pay it forward."

"Pay it what?" Mrs. Walker quizzed. Then Paul explained to her about paying it forward by doing something nice and unexpected for someone else, and then asking that person to do the same for another. As Paul cut her grass, Mrs. Walker couldn't stop smiling and thinking what a nice boy Paul was. Later that day, Mrs. Walker also found an opportunity to do something nice and pay it forward.

And so it was that the paying it forward begun that morning by Mr. Clark at the pharmacy continued all day long—indeed, all week long, as person after person passed on one good deed after another.

Follow-up: Ask the children if they have heard of "paying it forward." (You might remind them that there is a good movie by that name.) Explore different good deeds that each one might do in paying it forward.

23

A Friend Jodi

We Are Supposed to Help One Another

Scripture: Acts 3:1–10 GNT

Object for Sharing: A wheelchair

Presentation: This story will work well on a Sunday when persons with disabilities are being remembered.

Today I would like to tell you about someone named Jodi. Jodi was a classmate of Mr. Hammer, someone who writes a lot of children's sermons, when he was in college. Mr. Hammer and Jodi had some religion classes together.

On the campus of the college they attended are a lot of buildings. And the buildings are far apart, spread out over a large area. And some of the buildings are high up on hills, and some of them are down low in valleys.

Now, the reason this is important is because there was something special about Jodi. Jodi had a condition called cerebral palsy. Jodi couldn't walk, so he got around campus in a wheelchair. Remember I said the buildings on campus were spread far and wide, and some were on hills and some were down low? Well, it wasn't easy for Jodi to get from one building to the next. Mr. Hammer often would see Jodi struggling in his wheelchair to make it across campus in time for his next class. It was really difficult in the wintertime. His hands got really cold trying to turn the wheels on his chair.

So whenever Mr. Hammer happened to see Jodi and he was going the same way, Mr. Hammer would try to help him. He would say, "Jodi, would you like some company?" And by saying that, he was offering to push Jodi where he needed to go for his next class.

Well, Mr. Hammer says he probably did not help out Jodi nearly as much as he could have. He later wished he had helped him more. But we all can learn from our experiences, if we want to, can't we?

I think one of the main reasons that we are here on earth is to be a help to one another. So in the future, when we see someone in a wheelchair that could use a little bit of help, I hope you will remember the story about Mr. Hammer and his friend, Jodi.

Follow-up: To help children appreciate the difficulties those with handicaps face, lead them in an exercise of trying to maneuver around the building in a wheelchair.

24

Go, Fly a Kite!

Although We Cannot See It, There Is an Unseen Power We Call "God"

Scripture: John 3:8 GNT

Object for Sharing: A kite

Presentation: This lesson will work well in the springtime when many people think about flying kites, or during the season of Pentecost

---

Do any of you happen to have one of these? (Hold up the kite for all to see.). This is the time of the year when we think about flying kites, isn't it?

There is an old story about a child who was in a big city park one windy day flying a kite. The wind was just right for taking the kite way up in the air. It was a cloudy day, and there were a lot of low-hanging clouds in the sky. The kite kept going, and going, and going way up in the sky. The child was lucky to have a really big roll of strong string. Finally, the kite went so far up into the sky that it could no longer be seen. But the child held tight onto the string and never let go.

A man came along and saw the child standing there holding onto the string, but he could not see the kite. So he said to the child, "What are you doing?"

And the child replied, "I am flying a kite."

"But how do you know you are flying a kite?" the man asked. "You can't see it."

And so, the child responded, "But I can still fill the kite tugging on the string."

You know, that is sort of the way it is God. We believe that there is a Power in the world that we cannot see with our eyes. But we can sort of feel its tug. That Power most people call God.

In one place Jesus compared this Power, God, to the wind. You can't see the wind. But you can feel it. And you can see how the wind changes things around us. So it is with God.

As with the child holding onto the string, even though the kite could no longer be seen, so it is with the Power we call God. We may not be able to see God with our eyes, but we may still fill the tug of God on our hearts and see God's impact on the people and world around us.

Follow-up: Assist the children in assembling inexpensive kites for everyone. Then discuss kite safety (the importance of staying away from power lines, etc.).

25

In Search of the Perfect Dad

All Dads (and Moms) Sometimes Make Mistakes

Scripture: Colossians 3:13 GNT

Object for Sharing: A glass of milk and small rug or carpet remnant

Presentation: This story will work best on Father's Day. At the beginning of the story, "accidently" knock over the glass of milk on the rug.

Oh, look. I have spilled a glass of milk. Well, that reminds me of a story.

One day the son of the house spilled something on the white carpet in his room. The family had not lived in their new house long, and the carpet was almost like new. The dad got really upset and yelled at his son, "How could you do such a thing? Look at our new carpet! It is ruined!" Well, the son felt really terrible, and father later felt terrible about yelling too.

A couple of weeks later, the father spilled the same kind of thing on the carpet in another room of the house, staining it just as badly there as his son had in the other room. Now the father really felt terrible. He had yelled at his son for making a mistake, and now he had done the very same thing. But this time no one yelled at him like he had yelled at his son.

There was just one thing to do: the father went to his son's room, knocked on the door, and asked if he could come in. When he did, the father said, "Son, I want to apologize for yelling at you at few weeks ago for staining the carpet. I was wrong, and I want you to forgive me." The father determined that from that day forward, he would try to never yell at his children like that again.

You see, there are two lessons we can learn from this story. First, no father or mother is perfect. All mothers and fathers make mistakes. It is important that children understand that. Someday when you all grow up, if you become fathers and mothers, you will make mistakes too.

And the second lesson we learn from this story is that, just as the father learned from his mistake and determined that he would try to never yell at his children like that again for making mistakes, all of us can learn from our mistakes and determine to do better in the future.

So today, on Father's Day, remember that your Dad (and Mom) is only human. As much as all of us would like for our parents to be absolutely perfect, there hasn't been a perfect human parent yet. But we learn to love each other anyway.

Follow-up: Lead the children in making cards for their dads (and moms too, if appropriate), expressing gratitude for their parent's admirable qualities.

26
A Big Fish Tale
Jonah Teaches Us to Love Our Enemies

Scripture: Jonah summarized, GNT

Object for Sharing: A stuffed whale or picture of a big fish

Presentation: Although this story could work well at any time, especially when love for enemies is the theme, it will also work well in the summertime.

Does anyone remember the story of Jonah in the Bible? What happened to Jonah? He got swallowed by a big fish, didn't he?

Why did Jonah get swallowed by a big fish? While he was trying to run from God, he got tossed out of a boat while out at sea.

What was it that God wanted Jonah to do? God wanted Jonah to go preach to the people of Nineveh, a town a bit smaller than Knoxville, Tennessee.

But Jonah didn't want to go to preach to the people of Nineveh. Why do you suppose that was? Jonah looked upon the people of Nineveh as his enemies. But you know what? Jonah learned that God not only loved the people of Nineveh, those Jonah thought were his enemies, but God loved all the animals in Nineveh as well!

One of the biggest lessons we learn from the story of Jonah is God wants to us to try to find a way to love our enemies, perhaps those children at school that we don't think of as our friends. Sometimes those who we were thought were our enemies can end up being very good friends.

Hey, I hope that this summer you get to go to a zoo or an aquarium and see some really big fish.

Follow-up: Perhaps as a fun summer activity, a group trip to a local aquarium could be planned.

Annotated Resources

Anderson, Herbert, and Edward Foley. *Mighty Stories, Dangerous Rituals: Weaving Together the Human and the Divine.* San Francisco: Jossey-Bass, 1998.

Discusses the power of religious ritual and myth and how they help us create and express meaning. Shows how ritual and myth connect the human and divine.

Bettelheim, Bruno. *The Uses of Enchantment: The Meaning and Importance of Fairy Tales.* New York: Alfred A. Knopf, 1976.

An invaluable resource in the theory of how children's tales should arouse curiosity, stimulate the imagination, help children discover their self-identity and deal with inner conflicts, and confront their fears and problems.

Cameron, Julia. *The Artist's Way.* New York: G. P. Putnam's Sons, 1992.

Cameron seeks, through practical guidance, to bring out the creative energy, what she refers to as "God energy," that is within all of us.

Campbell, Joseph. With Bill Moyers. *The Power of Myth.* New York: Doubleday, 1988.

This work highlights exactly what the title suggests: the power of religious myths. Much is said about the hero that "lurks in each one of us."

Coles, Robert. *The Spiritual Life of Children.* Boston: Houghton Mifflin, 1990.

A wealth of wisdom has been gleaned and shared from Coles' interviews with hundreds of children from a number of religious backgrounds. This work reveals the great depth of thought in religious matters that children are capable of when given a chance to express themselves.

Estes, Clarissa Pinkola, ed. *Tales of the Brothers Grimm.* New York: Quality Paperback Book Club, 1999.

In her introduction, Estes discusses soul life, innate ideals, and universal thoughts. A good resource for those interested in universal thoughts and archetypes.

Fahs, Sophia L. *Jesus the Carpenter's Son.* Boston: Beacon Press, 1945.

Fahs uses the imagination (and indirectly encourages the modern presenter of children's sermons) to fill in the blanks and address the "What ifs" that surround the life of Jesus.

———. *Today's Children and Yesterday's Heritage.* Boston: Beacon Press, 1952.

In this work Fahs stresses the importance of a child's self-worth, the child's sense of relationship with the larger world, the need to "feel the Mystery of Life," and the interdependence of all life.

Groome, Thomas H. *Christian Religious Education.* Harper Collins, 1980.

Groome speaks of the importance of lived faith, becoming what we are called to become, and nurturing human freedom and creativity.

Hammer, Randy. *Everyone a Butterfly: 40 Sermons for Children*. Boston: Skinner House, 2004.

In addition to forty children's sermons that follow the church year beginning in September and ending in June, this collection includes an introduction that discusses the theory of sermon preparation for children and what makes for a "successful" children's sermon.

———. *The Shining Light: 26 Children's Sermons with Activities*. Cleveland: Pilgrim Press, 2010.

The introduction focuses on inspiration and where children's sermons come from.

———. *The Singing Bowl: 26 Children's Sermons with Activities*. Cleveland: Pilgrim Press, 2009.

The introduction suggests different places to look for children's sermons.

———. *The Talking Stick: 40 Children's Sermons with Activities*. Cleveland: Pilgrim Press, 2007.

Following the same format as the present volume, the forty stories and lessons in *The Talking Stick* generally follow the church calendar. A number of them acquaint listeners with historic figures, such as Brother Lawrence, Martin Luther, and Phyllis Wheatley. The stories encourage respect for everyone created in the divine image and seek to instill such positive qualities as service, hospitality, unity, stewardship of the earth, truthfulness, peacemaking, and the like. The introduction is titled "How do children's sermons come about?"

Handford, S. A., trans. *Aesop's Fables*. New York: Penguin, 1994.

In the introduction, Handford discusses the "common-sense and folk wisdom" at the heart of stories and fables.

Harris, Maria. *Fashion Me a People.* Louisville: Westminster John Knox Press, 1989.

Harris notes the importance of spending time alone "in the company of the Divine."

Jordan, Jerry Marshall. *Filling Up the Brown Bag* (a children's sermon how-to book). New York: Pilgrim Press, 1987.

An invaluable resource, Jordan stresses the importance of letting children know they are loved and wanted, nurturing within them an awareness of God, instilling within them a sense of self-worth and a positive self-image, encouraging children to stretch themselves and reach their full potential, and sparking their imaginations by getting them to say "I see!"

Lipman, Doug. *Improving Your Storytelling: Beyond the Basics for All Who Tell Stories in Work or Play.* Atlanta: August House, 1999.

A work that goes beyond the basics for storytellers, this is a good resource for those who seek to perfect the storytelling craft.

MacDonald, Margaret Read. *The Story-Teller's Start-Up Book: Finding, Learning, Performing and Using Folktales.* Little Rock, Ark.: August House, 1993.

A very helpful work that gives practical guidance on finding, preparing, and telling folktales and other stories.

Rogers, Fred. *Play Time.* Philadelphia: Running Press, 2001.

A good resource, most notably for preschoolers, for planning follow-up activities utilizing common household objects. Encourages children's use of imagination and creativity.

———. *You Are Special.* Philadelphia: Running Press, 2002.

A tiny pocket book of timeless wisdom that reinforces the truth that everyone is special, a concept that can easily be worked into many children's sermons.

Sawyer, Ruth. *The Way of the Storyteller.* New York: Penguin, 1970.

This work is a well-known classic on the art of storytelling that should be read by everyone who has a real interest in storytelling.

Silf, Margaret, ed. *Wisdom Stories from around the World.* Cleveland: Pilgrim Press, 2003.

Although written primarily from an adult viewpoint, many of these wonderful stories can be adapted for use with children.

Wagner, Betty Jane. *Dorothy Heathcote: Drama as a Learning Medium.* Revised ed. Portland, Me.: Calendar Islands Publishers, 1999.

Although written as a resource for leading children in drama, this is also a good resource—especially the first half—on how to physically lead children's sermons. Discusses the discovery of human experience, reaching a deeper insight, and helping children catch a vision of the wider world, as well as the importance of tapping the energy of the human spirit and valuing human achievement.

White, William R. *Stories for Telling: A Treasury for Christian Storytellers.* Minneapolis: Augusburg, 1986.

In addition to providing some good introductory material on storytelling in ministry, this work shares a great number of stories, folktales, and fables from a variety of sources that can be used or adapted for children's sermons.

Supply List

Chapter 1: The Dancing Stones

- Bowl of small, smooth stones, one for each child
- Stone polisher

Chapter 2: Something to Show the Way

- Small compass for each child
- One backpack

Chapter 3: A Lock without a Key

- Big padlock (not a combination padlock)
- A few keys without locks
- A small luggage lock (and key) for each child

Chapter 4: A Basket Case

- Handmade baskets
- Basket weaving materials and/or strips of construction
- Paper and paste

Chapter 5: Whose Job Is It?

- Large pitcher or punch bowl filled with water

Chapter 6: Looking Down or Looking Around?

- Piece of paper money

Chapter 7: Preparing the Manger

- Small basket
- Small bag of straw for each child
- Different pictures of the nativity
- Instructions for preparing the manger

Chapter 8: The Advent Wreath

- Advent wreath
- Green play dough
- Birthday or Hanukah candles

Chapter 9: Hand-drawn Gifts

- Variety of Christmas cards
- Cardstock and crayons, markers, or paints

Chapter 10: Away in a Manger

- Manger bed and doll
- Paper and crayons, markers, or paints

Chapter 11: Stocking Surprise

- Woman's stocking
- Chocolate gold coins

Chapter 12: January: Looking Back, Looking Forward

- Picture of Janus

Chapter 13: Turn on Your Light

- Windup flashlight

Chapter 14: Be Careful What You Say

- Plastic or real parrot in a cage

Chapter 15: Making Things Right

- Old, worn, weathered book

Chapter 16: In Search of Happiness

- Backpack containing snacks and water bottle

Chapter 17: The Great Knitter

- Knitted or crocheted article of clothing, preferably a shawl

Chapter 18: Climbing Out of a Hole

- Picture of a donkey

Chapter 19: Unexpected Beauty from Ugly Surroundings

- Photograph or painting of a lotus blossom

Chapter 20: Wave Those Pom-Poms

- High school or college pom-poms or shakers
- Palm branches

Chapter 21: Surprising Flowers

- Photograph of a desert wildflower

Chapter 22: Pay It Forward

- Large water toy

Chapter 23: A Friend Jodi

- Wheelchair

Chapter 24: Go, Fly a Kite!

- Kite, as well as one for each child

Chapter 25: In Search of the Perfect Dad

- Glass of milk
- Small rug or carpet remnant

Chapter 26: A Big Fish Tale

- Stuffed whale or photograph of large fish

About the Author

Randy Hammer

Randy Hammer has over thirty years of experience in pastoral ministry. He has worked with children in Vacation Church School, outdoor ministry, and of course, during the children's sermon time. His number one passion in ministry has been the preparation and delivery of sermons. Other passions include writing poetry and devotional materials, woodworking, and spending time with his wife, children, and their grandchildren.

He is the author of *Dancing in the Dark: Lessons in Facing Life's Challenges with Courage and Creativity* (1999, The Pilgrim Press), *Everyone a Butterfly: Forty Sermons for Children* (2004, Skinner House), *The Talking Stick: 40 Children's Sermons with Activities* (2007, The Pilgrim Press), *52 Ways to Ignite Your Congregation...Practical Hospitality* (2009, The Pilgrim Press), *The Singing Bowl: 26 Children's Sermons with Activities* (2009, The Pilgrim Press), and *The Shining Light: 26 Children's Sermons with Activities* (2009, The Pilgrim Press). Additionally, Randy is co-author of *What's So Amazing about Polar Bears: Teaching Kids to Care for Creation* (2011, The Pilgrim Press), and *God's Blue Earth: Teaching Kids to Celebrate the Sacred Gift of Water* (2013, The Pilgrim Press).

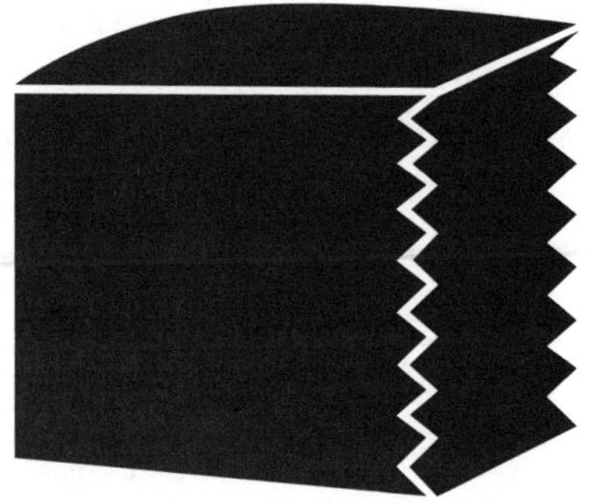

Other books from The Pilgrim Press

The Talking Stick
40 Children's Sermons with Activities

Randy Hammer
ISBN 978-0-8298-1761-4
paper/96 pages/$15.00

Show Me a Picture
30 Children's Sermons Using Visual Arts

Phyllis Vos Wezeman and Anna L. Liechty
ISBN 0-8298-1636-4
paper/96 pages/$12.00

Tell Me a Story
30 Children's Sermons Based on Best-Loved Books

Phyllis Vos Wezeman and Anna L. Liechty
ISBN 0-8298-1635-6
paper/96 pages/$12.00

Wipe the Tears
30 Children's Sermons on Death

Phyllis Vos Wezeman, Anna L. Liechty,
and Kenneth R. Wezeman
ISBN 0-8298-1520-1
paper/96 pages/$10.00

Taste the Bread
30 Children's Sermons on Communion

Phyllis Vos Wezeman, Anna L. Liechty,
and Kenneth R. Wezeman
ISBN 0-8298-1519-8
paper/96 pages/$10.00

Touch the Water

30 Children's Sermons on Baptism

Phyllis Vos Wezeman, Anna L. Liechty,
and Kenneth R. Wezeman

ISBN 0-8298-1518-X
112 pages/paper/$10.00

To order these or any other books from The Pilgrim Press call or write to:

The Pilgrim Press
700 Prospect Avenue East
Cleveland, Ohio 44115-1100

Phone orders: 1-800-537-3394 • Fax orders: 216-736-2206

Please include shipping charges of $6.00 for the first book and $1.00 for each additional book.
Or order from our web sites at www.pilgrimpress.com and www.ucpress.com.

Prices subject to change without notice.